SUMMARY OF

COUNTDOWN

1945

THE EXTRAORDINARY STORY OF THE ATOMIC BOMB AND THE 116 DAYS THAT CHANGED THE WORLD

BY CHRIS WALLACE
WITH MITCH WEISS

Proudly Brought To You By
OneHour Reads

ISBN: 978-1-952639-20-3

Table of Contents

EXECUTIVE SUMMARY 5
COUNTDOWN: 116 DAYS... 7
   Key Takeaways 7
COUNTDOWN: 113 DAYS... 9
   Key Takeaways 9
COUNTDOWN: 105 DAYS... 12
   Key Takeaways 12
COUNTDOWN: 104 DAYS... 16
   Key Takeaways 16
COUNTDOWN: 103 DAYS... 19
   Key Takeaways 19
COUNTDOWN: 90 DAYS... 22
   Key Takeaways 22
COUNTDOWN: 70 DAYS... 25
   Key Takeaways 25
COUNTDOWN: 68 DAYS... 28
   Key Takeaways 28
COUNTDOWN: 66 DAYS... 30
   Key Takeaways 30
COUNTDOWN: 53 DAYS... 32
   Key Takeaways 32
COUNTDOWN: 49 days.. 34
   Key Takeaways 34
COUNTDOWN: 36 DAYS... 35
   Key Takeaways 35
COUNTDOWN: 35 DAYS... 37
   Key Takeaways 37
COUNTDOWN: 34 DAYS... 38
   Key Takeaways 38
COUNTDOWN: 21 DAYS... 40
   Key Takeaways 40
COUNTDOWN: 20 DAYS... 43
   Key Takeaways 43
COUNTDOWN: 19 DAYS... 45
   Key Takeaways 45
COUNTDOWN: 18 DAYS... 47
   Key Takeaways 47
COUNTDOWN: 17 DAYS... 49
COUNTDOWN: 16 DAYS... 51
   Key Takeaways 51
COUNTDOWN: 13 DAYS... 53
   Key Takeaways 53
COUNTDOWN: 12 DAYS... 55

Key Takeaways 55
COUNTDOWN: 11 DAYS 57
Key Takeaways 57
COUNTDOWN: 8 DAYS 58
Key Takeaways 58
COUNTDOWN: 6 DAYS 60
Key Takeaways 60
COUNTDOWN: 5 DAYS 62
Key Takeaways 62
COUNTDOWN: 4 DAYS 64
Key Takeaways 64
COUNTDOWN: 3 DAYS 66
Key Takeaways 66
COUNTDOWN: 2 DAYS 67
Key Takeaways 67
COUNTDOWN: 1 DAY 68
Key Takeaways 68
COUNTDOWN: 9 HOURS, 15 MINUTES 71
Key Takeaways 71
COUNTDOWN: 9 HOURS 72
Key Takeaways 72
COUTDOWN: 8 HOURS 73
Key Takeaways 73
COUNTDOWN: 7 HOURS 38 MINIUTES 74
COUNTDOWN: 7 HOURS, 10 MINUTES 75
Key Takeaways 75
COUNTDOWN: 7 HOURS 5 MINUTES 76
COUNTDOWN: 6 HOURS, 30 MINUTES 76
Key Takeaways 76
COUNTDOWN: 3 HOURS, 30 MINUTES 76
COUNTDOWN: 2 HOURS 15 MINUTES 77
COUNTDOWN: 51 MINUTES 77
COUNTDOWN: 25 MINUTES 77
Key Takeaways 77
COUNTDOWN: 10 MINUTES 77
COUNTDOWN: 3 MINUTES 78
COUNTDOWN: 1 MINUTE 78
COUNTDOWN: 58 SECONDS 78
COUNTDOWN: 43 SECONDS 78
COUNTDOWN: FIRESTORM 79
EPILOGUE 80

EXECUTIVE SUMMARY

Besides being an account of World War II, the book COUNTDOWN by Chris Wallace with Mitch Weiss is filled with golden life nuggets for anyone who wants to be a great leader to thrive in their office. It is also for individuals who suddenly find themselves entrusted with huge responsibilities.

In this book, you'll see an eyewitness account that gives your mind a vivid picture of the chronicles of the war. You'll find the thoughts running through the minds of great leaders such as Harry Truman, President of the United States, Winston Churchill, and Joseph Stalin, the leader of the Soviet Union. You'll also meet ordinary people like Ruth Sisson, Hideko Tamura, and other men and women who had a part to play in the legendary war between the US and Japan.

You'll understand the pressure that great leaders go through to make the best choices, even if people or history decides to turn against you. It helps you know how to compartmentalize your thoughts; do something you don't like regardless.

You'll understand that no great man or woman stands alone. They are all surrounded by their team, who give them the advice they need. You'll see the importance of family and why you should hold them in high esteem. Hold your friends close and your family and loved ones closer.

The demands of confidence, dependability, consistency, and trustworthiness will always be thrust on your shoulders every time. You must brace yourself and do what needs to be done.

You also understand how to become a good leader.

COUNTDOWN: 116 DAYS

April 12, 1945
Washington, D.C.

Key Takeaways

1. Carry out your duties faithfully
2. Family is important
3. Time waits for no one so always be prepared for responsibility.
4. Learn to look for the bright side in everything.
5. Correct mistakes immediately they happen.
6. The people who surround you and offer counsel can make or mar you.
7. Learn to relax and rest in the face of trouble especially when you don't know what to do.

If your duties need to be carried out with utmost secrecy, then, by all means, do this. Your life might just depend on it.

Learn all you need to learn as quickly as possible. Sometimes responsibility can be thrust on you without any prior notice, and you have to carry out your duties without error. This will be difficult for you if you aren't prepared.

Carry your family along when you're making important decisions. They should also be relevant to you. If you don't, they may not be there when you need them the most.

If you find out someone is addressing you in the wrong way, correct the person immediately. This is because some mistakes may go public, and then it may be difficult to correct such errors.

If you make a mistake, correct yourself and don't beat yourself up for it. Get over it and move on. It doesn't matter what the crowd keeps saying. Simply acknowledge your mistake, correct yourself, and move on.

Your counselors or advisers have a part to play in the decisions you make. Sometimes, they may want to take advantage of the situation, especially if you're new in a position, but let them know you have the final say in any decision that is made.

When you don't know what to do, don't panic. If you can't think of a solution immediately, do something to help you rest and relax. By doing this, you're rebooting your mind. This will help you think of possible solutions.

What happened on this day?

Vice President Harry Truman was urgently summoned to the white house. President Roosevelt was dead.

He summoned his wife and daughter to the White House.

Truman was sworn in as President. He reaffirmed his intention to pursue Roosevelt's agenda.

He was told of a secret project that was underway.

COUNTDOWN: 113 DAYS

April 15, 1945

Los Alamos, New Mexico

Key Takeaways

1. You need people who are smart around you.
2. No one wants a weak leader.
3. Always communicate with the people you lead.
4. When working with people, opt for the best.
5. Clarity is one important skill a leader needs.
6. Your background doesn't have to determine your future.
7. Acquiring skills can never be too much.
8. An open mind will give no room for peevishness.
9. Learn to work well with others.
10. A leader serves as a light in the dark for the people he or she leads.
11. Words are powerful. That's what people will remember you for.

Smart people with sharp minds can help you decipher a problem and deliver clear, concise solutions. Make sure they can think fast.

If you're going to be next in line after a person who lived as an exemplary leader, then you need to step up quickly. You need to know how to hold the faith and confidence of the people who look up to you.

Communication is important. You need to know how to use your words. The people you lead will always look up to you to lead them aright. It's your words that give them the confidence they need to stand firm in the face of trails and disarray.

The family you came from doesn't have anything to do with the future you're heading to as long as you build yourself, and you continue to grow. You can still serve as a role model to people irrespective of what you've been through.

If you have an opportunity to learn anything or acquire any skills, then, by all means, make sure you do it. It doesn't matter if its horseback riding, and you are a scientist; simply make use of every opportunity you get.

When you have an open mind, and you broaden your mind when you interact well with others, this will disallow peevishness. There will be no room for you to be dismissive to the point of rudeness.

Be friendly. This world is too big for you alone. Learn to open your heart to people and socialize with friends and colleagues.

It is the job of a leader to keep people going even when everything looks bleak, and people get tired or worried. Only a leader can convince everyone to keep going even under strict conditions.

For every place you find yourself, always give your best. Put in wholehearted and unselfish labors.

Words spoken to people can't be taken back. They will be entrenched in the memory of those who hear them. Some of the great leaders in the world are renowned not just because they made significant decisions but also because they used great words to communicate with the people they lead. Through their speeches, they marked their footprints on the sand of time.

What happened on this day?

Oppenheimer, the scientific director of the Manhattan Project who was intelligent and brilliant, learned about President Roosevelt's death.

He informed the scientist he led in creating 'the gadget' which was a terrifying new weapon of mass destruction of the president's death.

COUNTDOWN: 105 DAYS

April 23, 1945

Wendover, Utah

Key Takeaways

1. Let no one deter you from becoming who you want to be.
2. Before choosing your team, have a list of the qualities you want
3. There will always be opposition in your way. You would be surprised that some people who oppose you are only searching for a way to forge ahead, and you will give them the push they want.
4. Be ready to take risks.
5. Always be honest and tell the truth, no matter how it looks.
6. Obey instructions. If you've been sworn to secrecy, then keep your mouth shut.
7. Diligence is non-negotiable for every leader.
8. Irrespective of what you see or feel, remain courageous and fearless. This will help you hang on even if the whole world doesn't believe in you or if everyone believes you're doing the wrong thing.
9. Experience will always be useful. Experience will make you stronger.
10. Hold on to your dreams; don't let anyone take it away from you.
11. Don't be sentimental when making decisions.
12. Follow your instincts.

If you have to opportunity to choose your team, choose people who can complement you. They should be people who have the skills that you admire or skills you don't have. They should be people who can be taught, or they can quickly learn. They should also be able to teach others.

You only live once. If you know what you want and you're sure of it, go after it.

Sometimes the strongest opposition you may face will come from those who love you. They oppose you because they love you and want to keep you safe. It takes greater willpower, determination, and strength to be able to stand up to them.

If you're under immense pressure to learn or if your boss is making you do more than you're supposed to do, go ahead and do it. It may not make sense at the beginning, but it will eventually. It will be great if you yield the intended result, and you can only do this if you take the pain to learn.

Whatever you're putting together or producing should be the best. It doesn't matter if it's a product or a service or if you're running a small business. If you can do better, then be better; hold nothing back. Never be satisfied with what you have or where you are. It doesn't matter how long it will take to improve or to create a new design or strategy. Do all you can to get the best so you can stand out above all others.

Stay out of trouble, especially with law enforcement agents, so that you can have a criminal free record. Sometimes these things come back, and they can hinder you from promotions later in life.

As a leader, you need conflict resolution skills. This is because many conflicts, challenges, and bickering may end up at your desk. Without this skill, it may be challenging to keep those you lead under check as issues may always blow up out of proportion.

Every good leader must be an exceptional strategist and an expert in any mission they undertake. When you have a task before you, create strategies to handle such missions, and be thorough when putting the strategy into practice.

If you have the opportunity to encourage someone who shares his or her dreams with you, encourage that person, and don't hold back. You may be the only anchor and reason why the person moves forward and wouldn't give up with his dreams.

When an opportunity presents itself to you, take it, especially if your boss or someone you respect gives you a chance. Prove yourself with every opportunity you get; it will bring more opportunities your way.

Every leader must be balanced and fair. It allows you to make your decisions without thinking of old ties to people. You can make sound decisions that way, and that's how to choose the best people to work with you.

What happened on this day?

Colonel Paul Tibbets Jr. had to soothe the nerves of the Police who had arrested some of the men he led. He was running a complex secret military operation with hundreds of pilots, navigators, bombardiers, and support personnel. He and a few people knew what it was all about.

COUNTDOWN: 104 DAYS

April 24, 1945

Okinawa, Japan

Key Takeaways

1. Be a problem solver and optimist.
2. Be determined to follow the path you have chosen for yourself no matter what comes your way.
3. Consistency is required of everyone who wants to be a leader.
4. Your life isn't a mistake. It may seem like you have defects, but don't let it determine the person you will become.
5. When you need to take steps, take intentional actions, and be fast about it.
6. Take your training seriously.
7. Everyone who is a part of your team is essential.
8. Work well with people.
9. Whatever you know will prove useful later.
10. Be like the baseball manager who's won ten games wearing the same dirty shirt, and he's not going to take that shirt off no matter how much it smells until he makes progress.

Training can never be too much or too long. It might seem like it's taking forever initially, but you'll find out that it is a lifesaver much later.

Ensure that before you undertake any task, you are fit physically, emotionally, and mentally.

Don't be scared when you meet hostility or disagreement along the way or during your training. It will eventually make you stronger. Be resilient, strong, and courageous in the face of trouble and hardship.

No matter how rigorous the training may be, just do all you can to survive. Survival is essential. What doesn't kill you will eventually make you stronger.

Remember that you can only survive if you take your lessons seriously. Every lesson is essential. Sometimes you need to watch and learn. At other times you will need to listen and learn. At other times you learn through experience. At other times you will need to ask questions. The baseline is that you should learn in every possible way.

For your training to be complete, learn to work well with your teammates. You will need each other, not just during your training but afterward.

Keep to the rules you're given in any place you find yourself. Don't take anything for granted.

Always encourage yourself no matter how you feel. If you think things are difficult in a particular phase or position, wait till you get out of that phase or you're promoted. You'll realize there are more complicated tasks or responsibilities in your way, and then you'll appreciate the previous step. If you don't believe, think of the most challenging things in your way five years ago. Are they still as difficult as they were five years ago? If the answer is no, then be encouraged and know that the pain and hardship will pass.

Even when you're faced with troubles and hardships, try to encourage and help those who are around you. This is because everyone needs it, and that may be the only reason why someone around you refuses to quit.

Don't be scared to get dirty. If everyone refuses to go further, take the lead, and go deeper. No knowledge is a waste. Be the one who isn't carried away by the previous successes.

What happened on this day?

Commander Draper Kauffman's 'frogmen' were returning from another reconnaissance mission. He received his men. He was in charge of training the men.

<u>COUNTDOWN: 103 DAYS</u>

April 25, 1945
Washington, D.C.

Key Takeaways

1. Be a decisive leader.
2. Always be prepared. You never know where you'll find yourself in a short while.
3. Never look down on yourself no matter where you're coming from.
4. Have a track record of being honest and consistent.
5. Don't settle where you are. Always progress and grow.
6. You need a trusted adviser in your life.
7. Never say never; don't rule yourself out of any position because you feel you don't have prospects.
8. Family is important. It is also important to surround yourself with the right people.
9. Self-confidence and knowledge of your work will do the same work manipulation will do.
10. As a leader, understand the importance of your decisions as the lives of the people you lead depend on the choices you make.

Immediately you get into a position, or assume a new role, make the crucial changes that you need to make in that office. You don't have to wait because something else can happen.

Always have a central point of success or failure in your life. This person should be able to tell you the truth and give you candid advice when you need it. The person can look you straight in the eye and inform you when you're wrong, give you a critique, and also encourage you when you're down. This person can be your spouse or partner, a parent, a child, a childhood friend, a trusted aide, or anyone who can do this for you. You can pay the person to do the job, so they take the role seriously.

Be proactive. Think in advance and decide in advance of thinking. Be someone who can think through plans and decisions even before the policies or decisions are made.

As much as you want to be a reputable leader, make sure you're smart, gregarious, and hardworking.

Understand the tenets of your profession. Be rugged and polite at the same time. Be a gentleman or a lady or someone who is always decent.

You don't have to be intimidating to make your presence felt by everyone. Do your job and be real with everyone. You don't have to be overbearing, brash, controlling, or manipulative to be in charge.

Trust your instinct as a leader. You need to know when to change grounds or give your approval or disapproval of every decision that was made from your predecessors. Understand that some decisions can go awry, and some can be successful. Nevertheless, the final decision is in your hands, and you will take the applause or fall for every decision made on your behalf or every decision that passes through you.

What happened on this day?

Everyone noticed Harry Truman was a decisive leader.

On August 25, secretary of war Henry Stimson handed him a short, typewritten memorandum about the atomic bomb they were working on. General Groves was involved, Leo Szilard came up with the idea of the bomb, and Albert Einstein was also involved.

Truman was told the bomb was so powerful that it could destroy the whole world.

COUNTDOWN: 90 DAYS

May 8, 1945

Washington, D.C

Key Takeaways

1. Be a leader who can laugh in the face of pressure and tough times.
2. Be approachable as a leader
3. Learn to give credit to whom credit is due.
4. Use your words beautifully and wisely.
5. Build relationships with people. You never know what they are going through, and they may just need your ears. Sometimes people don't care how much you know till they know how much you care.
6. Life can be a routine. Make sure you don't get bored. Learn to create something beautiful for yourself. You can do this by reading, socializing, getting a job, or acquiring a new skill.
7. Worry and anxiety do nothing helpful. It keeps the mind in a state of fear, and you will notice that you don't enjoy your life. Worrying never produces anything productive. It just eats up your mind with ideas that may not be true while taking you away from the present.

Be a leader everyone can speak to without fear. Sometimes the answers you need may not be with your immediate team members. The 'eureka' you need may come from the janitor or security officials.

As a leader, you may be called upon to speak at any time. Learn to speak the right words at any time. Your words must consistently be encouraging and uplifting. You can read speeches from different world leaders or inspiring quotes at various times to give you a wealth of words that you can quickly draw your words from.

Don't just be a leader who is interested in giving the people instructions. Get involved in the lives of the people you lead. Sometimes, they may be experiencing a devastating loss, or they may be going through tough times. Many people appear at work daily, but no one knows the battle each person is fighting on their own. Take it upon yourself as a leader to know the people who work with you and get interested in their lives without meddling in their affairs.

Open your heart to people. It doesn't matter if times are difficult and you've met a lot of bad people, there are still good people out there, and there's someone meant for you among the people you meet daily.

Whatever work you find yourself doing, do it faithfully. It might be a lifesaver to a family, a friend, or someone you don't know.

Life comes with anxiety and worries. You have to learn to live above it. Find something to keep the tension away. It can be music, dancing, working, learning a skill, enjoying beautiful landscapes and nature, or any other thing that piques your interest.

Learn to look at the cheerful side of life. Gratitude keeps anxiety and worries away. This is when you take your time to count the good things that happen to you, it encourages you to look forward t the bright side of life, and you see that the future isn't bleak or filled with dread, which is what worry and anxiety makes you think.

What happened on this day?

President Truman announced Hitler's death and the German laying down of arms.

Ruth Sisson was glad the Nazi's surrendered. She expected that her fiancé, who was in the army, would come home. She worked as a cubicle operator at the Army plant.

COUNTDOWN: 70 DAYS

May 28, 1945

Washington, D.C.

Key Takeaways

1. Your skill shouldn't be an excuse for lack of order or inappropriate behavior.
2. Aim to be the best and excel in all you do.
3. Do your work to the best of your abilities
4. Always get your facts right
5. Speak up if you know something helpful
6. Before you judge someone, listen to their side of the story first.
7. Always make in-depth plans about any action you plan to carry out.

When you're doing your work, do it as if the fate of the world rests in your hand. That's the way to carry out your responsibilities dutifully.

Progression is part of life. The fact that you conquered one obstacle doesn't mean all challenges have been overcome. Even as you celebrate, prepare for the next obstacle ahead.

It is crucial to get your facts right because they help you strategize better when you're planning. No information is a waste.

Sometimes speaking up can be a lifesaver. A person, the person's work, a plan, or a place could be in danger, and you can save lives by speaking up.

The way people react to issues can be different as there are two ways to respond to any problem. A person can react in different ways: it can be objectively, by giving facts and stating what went wrong. In this case, people deter you from getting involved in brawls, fights, or war. People can also react subjectively when the issue at hand affects that individual directly. This makes the individual pragmatic about the issue at hand.

Without making plans and creating strategies, all you are trying to do may never work out. You need a step by step strategy to ascertain if all your well-written plans can be actualized.

To create and implement strategies, you need a wise person who knows something about everything. The individual doesn't have to be someone who is easily noticed, and it's a plus if the person can get along with other team members. You simply need someone like this on your team.

What happened on this day?

Colonel Tibbets attended a high-level Pentagon meeting, and Beser was meant to be there with him. He was running late.

Five potential targets were chosen as places to strike: Kyoto, Hiroshima, Yokohama, Kokura, and Niigata. Stimson saved Kyoto.

Beser joined the meeting later. He was one of the best radar men in the country. He figured they were building an atomic bomb.

COUNTDOWN: 68 DAYS

May 30, 1945

Kimita, Japan

Key Takeaways

1. Kids are the major casualties of war
2. As a leader, learn how to troubleshoot on issues before they come up. Look for a way to resolve problems before they blow up into significant issues.
3. Never hide information from the people you lead. Don't give them half-truths as the whole truth.
4. Provide the people you lead with all they need to make their work and their lives as easy and as smooth as possible.
5. Children are the leaders of tomorrow. They are the future still in the stages of growth and development. Parents and leaders should do all they can do to make life worth living for them.

In every war, kids are on top of the list of those most affected. They are displaced, they starve, they can be used or sold as slaves, and they go through different horrors that will affect them as long as they live.

Peace-keeping and conflict resolution is an essential skill for every leader. Consider all the vulnerable groups before you make any decisions to go to war.

Respect the culture of people. It carries their beliefs and values. It will determine the perspective people of a particular culture have about you.

There's nothing as terrible as a government or leader that takes advantage of their people. As a leader, never make decisions that favor you but leave your people exposed. Some leaders do this and take advantage of the vulnerable state of their people by deceiving them.

What happened on this day?

Hideko Tamura and her friend Miyoshi went through their morning routine. They washed at the creek, dressed up in their school, performed their morning sutra, chanted the *Namu Amida Butsu* chant, and went for breakfast.

She and the other kids were evacuated from Hiroshima to Kimita for safety. Still, they were used for manual labor instead of the provision and protection the government promised their families.

COUNTDOWN: 66 DAYS
June 1, 1945
Washington, D.C.

Key Takeaways

1. Never stick to the old-fashioned ways of doing things.
2. Peace is more cost-effective than war
3. There is no easy way to win.
4. War must be restrained within the bounds of humanity
5. As a leader, understand that the actions you take are strong enough to alter the entire course of civilization. This means there are no simple decisions, as every decision has its own impact and consequence.

Is war the best way to settle battles and conflicts? What is the economic impact of war? Have you weighed the environmental damage? What about the morality of employing such a devastating weapon against your fellow human beings? What if your child was there, would you still take a war/battle approach? Let questions such as this influence your decisions.

As a leader, what's more important? The rush to beat your competition at their game or the need to consider the wellbeing and preservation of other human beings like yourself?

Before you make any decision, ask yourself this question: if my family or kids were involved in this situation, how would I handle this crisis and make this decision? Your answer should determine your actions.

What happened on this day?

The American people were tired of war, but the President told Congress there's no easy way to win in Japan, which meant there would be more casualties of war.

Stimson created a new policy; guidelines for the proper use of nuclear weapons in war and peacetime. He established an Interim Committee for this cause. The interim committee met four times in May and reconvened June 1 to discuss the bomb's potential destructive power and the effect it would have on the Japanese will to fight.

They finally agreed and sent a message to Truman that:

- The atomic bomb should be unleashed as soon as possible.
- It should be unleashed in such a way that houses and other buildings would be affected.
- It must be unleashed out of the blue.

COUNTDOWN: 53 DAYS

June 14, 1945

Omaha Nebraska

Key Takeaways

1. Be someone who can keep a cool head in harrowing situations.
2. Learn to work with all kinds of people.
3. Sometimes you need to stay in your own league to save yourself.
4. Be someone who understands the rules and sticks to it no matter the cost.

When you're meeting people or working with people, do this with an open mind as it will help you when you're interacting with them. Understand that the family and environment in which you grew up as well as the circumstances that formed you is different from what other people went through. This is why no two people can ever be the same.

Sometimes the person who aids your work or the person you need might be someone who is the direct opposite of you.

Before you take an action that is only meant to save your head, think about the effect on you, your team, your brand, or your organization. Is your action worth it?

Don't be focused on unimportant things such as who likes you or who doesn't. Focus on the tasks before you and the job you were employed to undertake.

If you're undergoing training and it appears to be frustrating, redundant, and boring, don't leave the work. Consider it a form of training.

What happened on this day?

Beser was an excellent pilot, and Tibbets chose him.

COUNTDOWN: 49 days

June 18, 1945

Washington, D.C.

Key Takeaways

1. It's always safer to have people you love around you.
2. Make sure you state your opinion

It's good to ponder on the various ways to reach your target end. If you're aiming for peace, what's the best way to go by it? Is war the only way out?

Your voice may not be the loudest in the room, but you can still state your opinion. There's nothing wrong with that even if it seems as though everyone is against your idea.

What happened on this day?

The president convened a meeting with his war cabinet, Joint Chiefs of Staff and top civilian officials from the War Department. The meeting was to discuss how to force Japan's unconditional surrender and end World War II. They weighed all options and the cost of invading Japan, the projected casualties and losses on the American side.

The president ordered the Joint Chiefs to proceed with their plan to invade Kyushu.

COUNTDOWN: 36 DAYS

July 1, 1945

Los Alamos, New Mexico

Key Takeaways

1. Even if you're friendly as a leader, never tolerate failure and delay.
2. Always give your best shot and make sure your work is nothing less than perfect.
3. Every parent should encourage their child to be who they want to be.
4. When you're under pressure, you'll easily be on edge and exhausted.
5. Obstacles are part of life. Deal with it and defeat it.
6. Don't be deterred when people look down on you. Know what you want and go after it. Never allow anyone to put you out of your place. If you allow it for once, it will happen continually.
7. Don't be shy to ask questions. It's a sign of someone who's growing or someone who wants to know.
8. In whatever task or project you undertake, work without delay. Be as fast as you can.

Create a system to help you deal with pressure. Learn to take a break, relax, and rest amid pressure. As much as you can, don't allow the stress overwhelm you.

Don't allow anyone to treat you like a recluse. Refuse to be intimidated by anyone: superiors, colleagues, or people from other fields or spheres of life.

Stand for what you believe is right and defend it. It doesn't matter if everyone says you have no right to do it or you're only a woman; it's merely an obstacle, and obstacles are meant to be overcome.

Kids quickly pick up what they see. If they see your library and spend time there, it's easier for them to love reading than if you only gave them a bunch of instructions to read.

If no one believes in you or if everyone thinks you can't do it because you aren't good enough or because you're a woman, prove them wrong by showing them what you can do.

If you need help, ask for it. Don't be too shy or proud to do so. Sometimes your life and all you've worked for might depend on it.

What happened on this day?

The trinity explosion was set for July 16. Scientists were signing petitions to prevent the use of the bomb.

COUNTDOWN: 35 DAYS

July 2, 1945

Los Alamos, New Mexico

Key Takeaways

1. Working with people and sharing your work with them makes life easier.
2. Vouch for people with tested and trusted loyalty.

Learn to interact and build relationships with people because no one knows it all. You need people around you to help you. Cooperate and share knowledge with them as it can help you become better. Get involved in group discussions and groups that can help you grow.

No matter how close you are to people or how long you've worked with them, don't assume you can trust them if you don't know so much about them.

It's better to work with people than to work alone. This is because it fosters creativity, efficiency, and teamwork.

What happened on this day?

Groves made sure the atomic bomb project was kept a secret. He tried to screen the scientists on the project since they were foreign-born.

COUNTDOWN: 34 DAYS

July 3, 1945

Los Alamos, New Mexico

Key Takeaways

1. If your work is distinct, you'll always stand out.
2. You need a sharp and intelligent mind to get the information that's everyone doesn't have; usually, this kind of information is useful.
3. Don't judge people by their looks.
4. Your background shouldn't shape your future. You have to power to rewrite your story.
5. Curiosity is an important virtue that can make you a trailblazer and one of the most innovative people in your field.
6. Whenever you find an opportunity, think of the attendant risks involved, and if your instincts approve of it, go with it.
7. Before undertaking any task, keep the goal in mind. This will help you stay on track when you find out other information or when your enthusiasm overrides the job.
8. One way to live a fulfilled life is to do what you love.

Try to gain a broad perspective. Fit what you know into the larger picture. This will imply that you should read wide and interact with people from different departments or career.

You don't need to prove you're in charge or that you're the best in your field or department. Simply be good at what you do with no intention of proving a point. Make sure your work stands out, and you'll be recognized.

Don't be too quick to produce results. If you feel that there is information you lack or something isn't quite right, wait till you get all you need first. It's better to wait and give out the desired result than to give out an incomplete result.

Always be balanced. Learn to be creative but give room for laymen, professors, literate, and the illiterate to understand what you do. This means you do your work creatively while paying attention to every detail. This will give you an edge over others, but you must also understand that this will come with a level of pressure.

What happened on this day?

William Laurence was chosen as the journalist to report on the bomb.

COUNTDOWN: 21 DAYS

July 16, 1945

Potsdam Germany

Key Takeaways

1. No matter whom you meet and where you find yourself, just be yourself.
2. Don't allow yourself to be intimidated. Get to know what intimidates you; identify the triggers, your strengths and weaknesses, and get on top of the situation.
3. Self-confidence and resilience are important for any leader. Be a person of your word.
4. Develop a good working relationship with people.
5. No matter what amazes, excites or disappoints you, keep a clear head. Keep a balanced and objective view always.
6. With plans, optimism can make your ideas work out.

Know your strengths and your weaknesses. Be confident in your strength and wield it in your favor.

No matter how excited you are to meet a person or assume a new position, don't build high hopes until there's physical contact and an appraisal of the person or what you're going to do. Without this appraisal, there may be a disappointment.

Understand what helps you calm down and then follow it righteously. If it is journaling, exercising, music, or any skills you've acquired, try to do it as often as you can.

Be optimistic and realistic at the same time. If you create a plan for something to work, develop strategies to ensure that the project falls into place. If the plan doesn't work, think of a back-up plan.

In life, there will be two sides: good and bad, war and peace, great and evil. If you're on the good side, be careful that you don't become the evil you're trying to destroy.

What happened on this day?

The President woke up in Germany that morning on his first foreign trip as President.

He was there for the Postdam Conference with British Prime Minister Winston Churchill and Soviet premier Stalin. Truman was intimidated to be in the presence of these leaders.

The conference didn't kick off that day because Stalin didn't arrive.

The President took an unscheduled tour of Berlin, and he said he had never seen 'a more sorrowful sight nor witness retribution to the nth degree.'

The first nuclear weapon was to be tested in New Mexico, in the US and the President awaited word of the test.

Some people didn't believe the nuclear bomb 'Little Boy' would work while the 'Fat Man' wouldn't work.

The bomb worked perfectly well. Civilians were scared, but the army released a statement to reassure them they were safe.

COUNTDOWN: 20 DAYS

July 17, 1945

Potsdam, Germany

Key Takeaways

1. There's no other feeling like getting intended results on any task and hearing 'well done' from your boss.
2. Integrity is non-negotiable in leadership.
3. Be someone that everyone is willing to go the extra mile for.
4. Be straightforward, reliable, honest and smart as hell.
5. Don't be afraid or too intimidated to state what you think. If you need to be blunt about it to get your results, then by all means be blunt.
6. Responsibility can suddenly be thrust on you so be prepared. This can help you steer conversation and decisions in your favor.

Create plans to work with. This will let you know how much you've accomplished and what you haven't done.

Be concerned about the people you lead. Care about them genuinely not only on work-related matters but also as regards their health and other areas of their lives.

Be consistent. Let your virtues to be known by everyone. Be someone that everyone can list out their qualities.

If your decision is going to affect people's lives, you need to be able to understand those you work with. This will help you when you're strategizing, and it will inform you of potential opportunities and threats.

When working with people, have goals that you focus on to help you reach your destination. People can be selfish, but when there are goals that lead you to the required destination, it's easy to identify who can work with you to achieve these goals.

What happened on this day?

The President received word that the bomb test yielded a satisfactory result.

Truman named the meeting 'Terminal.' He told his other counterparts at the conference that he didn't play diplomatic games. He was ready to decide, not discuss.

Truman was pleased with the events of the day.

COUNTDOWN: 19 DAYS
July 18, 1945
Potsdam Germany

Key Takeaways

1. No two people are the same. If someone occupies an office, it doesn't mean the individual will act like the predecessor.
2. Take a deep breath and calm down when you're anxious.
3. If you're in the midst of people you don't trust, you can code messages for your own safety.
4. You can learn from your predecessor but you don't have to act the way they did.
5. Don't be totally dependent on people and the plans you make with them or the plans you think they will make. They may have their own plans that you may be unaware of.

Your competitive edge will come from your ability to begin a project, get the right people on the team to execute the project while ensuring they all work with the goal you had in mind.

In life, nothing is predictable, especially when you work with people. Everything may not work out just the way you want it to go. Be flexible when making plans and decisions.

When things don't go the way you want them to go, there's no need to panic or get angry. You accomplish nothing that way. Create new strategies and think of how to forge ahead and don't let anyone waste your time.

What happened on this day?

The President received a coded message on the full report on the bomb test.

He shared this news with Churchill, who was as delighted as he was. Churchill believed the supernatural weapon might be able to end the war in one or two violent shocks. They decided they should share the news with Stalin without divulging the details.

The President later became frustrated with the slow pace of great power diplomacy.

COUNTDOWN: 18 DAYS

July 19, 1945

Oak Ridge, Tennessee

Key Takeaways

1. War takes much more from us than we acknowledge or know.
2. Family can be the only support you have in trying times.
3. Make plans for the things you'll do when life goes back to normal.
4. Keep your true friends close and your loved ones closer. You'll always need them during the darkest times.

It's better to be quiet than to use the wrong words when trying to comfort people. Your demeanor, a gentle smile, or your silence can say more than a million words. In some cases, there are no words to lift a person's spirit.

In times of war and sadness, try to look on the bright side. Remember the things that made you happy and write out a list of the things that you're grateful for.

What happened on this day?

According to the news, US planes were turning Japanese cities into raging infernos, and Tokyo was reduced to rubble.

The Japanese emperor still didn't surrender.

Ruth Sisson thought about Lawrence her fiancé a lot. She was also worried her brothers would be drafted in the war. She spent most of her time in the factory she worked for.

COUNTDOWN: 17 DAYS
July 20, 1945
Potsdam, Germany

Key Takeaways

1. Follow your instincts.
2. Try to always remain in high spirits irrespective of all that's happening around you.
3. Keep your friends close and your family closer.
4. Don't waste time on issues that don't matter. Politely state your position and move on.

Those who stand out always have a different opinion. Express yours even if others don't agree.

Let your vision and goals be clear for everyone to see. It makes those who support it stick close to you, and those who don't can leave you.

What do you want to be remembered for? A man of peace, a man of war, a man who ushered in new technology that will alter human lives negatively or positively?

What happened on this day?

Truman was happy they hadn't been able to accomplish anything at the conference. He wanted the Soviets to join the fight to ensure victory regardless of possible long-term consequences.

His stand as regards the Japanese war was unconditional surrender.

Truman still had his doubts about using the bomb and if it would work in a war setting or if it would force the Japanese to surrender. He discussed strategy in the Pacific and whether to drop the bomb with Generals Dwight Eisenhower and Omar Bradley. Eisenhower had grave misgivings about the bomb, and he didn't want Stalin to join the war.

COUNTDOWN: 16 DAYS

July 21, 1945

Tinian

Key Takeaways

1. As much as you can, make life easier for your boss, colleagues and team members.
2. Build relationships with the people you work with. Be as friendly and as cordial as possible. This can save your life and work.
3. Learn to be patient. Things will eventually make sense.
4. Follow orders.
5. Don't assume you know people until you meet them.
6. Show and tell when you need to make your point known; don't shout or explode to make everyone understand your point.
7. Learn to work with the information and resources you have.
8. You have no reason to be proud. There will always be people who know much more than you do.
9. Don't overlook issues that will eventually lead to rancor and cause trouble. Confront it and deal with it for the good of the job.

Trust your boss or the one who makes the decisions no matter what you think or how the situation seems.

Sometimes, the people who are hard on you might just be protecting you.

When you're interacting with people, learn to control your anger. Anger will only make things worse. Go for a thoughtful approach and clearly state your feelings and sort out your indifferences.

What happened on this day?

Colonel Tibbets drilled his men harder since the bomb worked.

Lieutenants Jacob Beser, his best radar man, was grounded. Tibbets didn't want to lose him.

Brigadier General John Davies was intrigued by Tibbets group, but he didn't get along well with Tibbets. Tibbets sent three of his crews to one of Davies sessions, and Davies got to know how good they were.

General LeMay also didn't like Tibbets and wanted to give the atomic bomb mission to another unit. Blanchard was assigned to test the proficiency of Tibbets' team, and they gave Blanchard a ride he'll never forget. That ended the situation between Tibbets and General LeMay.

COUNTDOWN: 13 DAYS

July 24, 1945

Potsdam, Germany

Key Takeaways

1. Be willing to give people second chances
2. You must be able to think thoroughly and selflessly to make good decisions
3. Don't opt for the easiest solution. Opt for the best and most balanced decision in light of all the knowledge you have.
4. As a leader, learn to separate what you feel as a person from who you are as a leader.

Your decisions as a leader goes a long way, and it will never end with you. It will ignite in others the power to make the same decision.

Listen to your advisers and make sense out of what they are saying. Go through all your option before making a decision. That's the best way to make a balanced final decision.

As a leader, it is your responsibility to reason on behalf of others and make a choice that is for the best of all concerned individuals or parties.

What happened on this day?

Truman still wanted to give the Japanese one last chance to surrender. He was hoping he would never use it. He was looking for a way out which was to take the form of a carefully worded ultimatum to Tokyo to be issued by the three nations at war with Japan: the United States, Britain, and China as the Postdam Declaration.

The President acknowledged that the United States had discovered the most terrible bomb in the history of the world.

The target was for military objectives, soldiers, and sailors, not women and children. This was why Kyoto or Tokyo wasn't chosen. The focus was on Hiroshima and Nagasaki.

U.S. forces killed more than 100,000 Japanese in Okinawa, and more than 100,000 were destroyed in Japanese cities, but there was no surrender from the Japanese.

The President informed Stalin of the bomb. Stalin sounded uninterested, but he was interested. He had a spy working as a physicist in Los Alamos named Klaus Fuchs.

COUNTDOWN: 12 DAYS

July 25, 1945

Los Alamos, New Mexico

Key Takeaways

1. There will be moral implications in war. Expect darkness, depression, sadness and similar emotions.
2. One great virtue of a leader is the ability to compartmentalize his or her thoughts.
3. There's a level of stress and exhaustion that comes with your responsibility and office. As you aim for new responsibilities, be prepared for it too.
4. Even if your team doesn't back you up, don't be too quick to give up.

Focus on each day and how to solve its challenges. Tomorrow will come with its problems and peculiar solutions. If you focus on tomorrow's challenges, you will be bogged down by fear, anxiety, worry, and depression.

Be prepared to deal with the effects of the decisions you make as a leader. If there will be inescapable damage, prepare to contain it.

Even when you have solved the challenges of today, tomorrow will still come with its challenges. Learn to stay in the present and not worry about the future.

Family is important. If you have one, keep them dear to your heart.

What happened on this day?

Scientists who were excited about the success of the bomb began to lose their excitement as the reality of the bomb's destruction dawned on them. They began to debate the morality of using atomic weapons. Some saw it as a trade-off while some felt guilty about it.

Oppenheimer didn't like it, but he was able to compartmentalize his thoughts. He gave instructions on how it was to be used.

Harry Truman wasn't able to get the thoughts about the bomb out of his mind. He understood the magnitude of his decision. This was why he sent warnings to the Japanese to surrender.

Churchill left the conference to return to London to hear the result of the general election.

COUNTDOWN: 11 DAYS

July 26, 1945

Tinian

Key Takeaways

1. There's nothing wrong with acquiring more knowledge from other fields to the extent of practicing in those newly acquired fields.
2. Sometimes you may not understand the instructions you receive but the intensity attached to these instructions require that you follow it. That should be enough for you.

What happened on this day?

Captain James Nolan and Major Robert Furman were on the USS Indianapolis. They were to guard the lead-like container, which contained $300 million worth of weapons-grade uranium-235 destined to fuel America's first combat-ready atomic bomb.

The Indianapolis dropped anchor half a mile off Tinian and winched the crate from the deck onto a landing craft.

Four days after delivering the uranium, the Indianapolis was torpedoed by a Japanese submarine. Only 317 of the 1,200 sailors on board survived.

Churchill lost the general elections, and Clement Attlee won.

COUNTDOWN: 8 DAYS
July 29, 1945
Tinian

Key Takeaways
1. Don't work with superstition or other negative feelings. Be patient until you know the truth.
2. Don't listen passively. Always pay attention to details as well as what you feel has been said or avoided.
3. To assume responsibility means you have to give up childish games and grow up.
4. Learn to be flexible with your team no matter how you feel about others.
5. You don't have to do so much to prove yourself.
6. As much as you can, verify the information and instructions you receive. This will prevent you from disappointment and heartbreaks.
7. Don't use a person's mistake to judge him for the rest of his life.

When you're in shock or under pressure, don't be quick to panic because you wouldn't think straight. Calm down and keep a level head so you can figure out what to do.

When you're leading a team of people, be honest with them, and give them the information they need. This way, they trust you, and they have less reason to panic.

Assumptions will not produce anything fruitful. It will only build resentment between you and your partners or colleagues. This can be harmful to any given task or project you're handling. Be precise and verify all thoughts.

Understand your feelings and see them as an indication of what you think. Emotions can sometimes be a figment of your imagination and not reality. You may feel someone is too brash and see it as a reason why the person wouldn't make the right decisions; in actuality, you may be wrong since you haven't tested the person's decision-making skills.

Harness the strength of your team. You need those who are young, willing to take risks, and swift to action just as you need those who are wise, take calculated steps, and are slow to act.

What happened on this day?

For the mission of the day, Lewis was flying behind the Strange Cargo piloted by Major James Hopkins. The bomb bay door opened, and a five-ton bomb dropped onto the runway. Lewis informed his crew of the development, and after the runway was clear, they headed on to their mission.

Tibbets congratulated Lewis when he arrived from his mission and told him he'd be flying the mission. Lewis felt Tibbets meant he would be piloting the plane.

COUNTDOWN: 6 DAYS
July 31, 1945
Potsdam Germany

Key Takeaways

1. Be a man of integrity whether people are watching you or not.

Before taking a decision that carries adverse effects, exhaust all options to make peace or reach a conclusion.

Have value for the lives of people, not just the people you lead but also the people who will directly or indirectly feel the effect of every decision you make.

What happened on this day?

President Truman was homesick.

On July 26, the Chinese sent their approval for the unconditional surrender of Japan.

The Postdam Declaration stated, 'The time has come for Japan to decide whether she will continue to be controlled by those self-willed militaristic advisers whose unintelligent calculations have brought the Empire of Japan to the threshold of annihilation or whether she will follow the path of reason.'

The United States got the message to the enemy by using warplanes to drop 600,000 leaflets across the Japanese homeland.

Two days later, Prime Minister Kantaro Suzuki announced that his government didn't consider the declaration of great importance. They showed their determination to fight on and launched a fresh wave of kamikaze suicide attacks against American ships.

On July 31, the President received another top-secret cable from Washington, which said, 'The time schedule on Groves' project (S-1) is progressing so rapidly that it is now essential that statement for release by you be available not later than Wednesday, 1 August'. This was the message the American team had worked on for weeks.

The President approved the suggestion.

COUNTDOWN: 5 DAYS
August 1, 1945
Tinian

Key Takeaways

2. When you're selecting your team, make sure all aspects are covered.
3. Set aside all personal differences for the goal or task ahead.
4. A leader with foresight and wisdom knows how to bring out the best in people.
5. Confidence, competency, dependability and consistency are non-negotiable for every leader who will stand out.
6. Don't assume that no one notices it when you give your best effort. One day, it will make sense.
7. Don't forget other factors that can affect the result of the effort you put into your work

Sometimes when your bosses push you hard and heap pressure on you, it's to bring out the best in you.

Always plan and create strategies. Create back up plans in case your initial plan doesn't work out. Make sure the ideas are clear and straight to the point, so it can be easy for anyone to follow it.

Always keep your cool even under pressure. Learn to relax, and don't be quick to show the anxiety and panic you feel inward.

What happened on this day?

The date to drop the bomb was any time after August 3.

Tibbets put the plan for the mission together. He chose the planes and his team.

COUNTDOWN: 4 DAYS

August 2, 1945

Potsdam

Key Takeaways

1. Go into any task with clear goals; it helps you know when you've met your target.
2. When meeting people, think of what you can learn from them. This helps you pay attention to details and focus on what you can learn.
3. You may not like where you are or the things that are happening around you but you must learn to endure because it will pass.

Everyone has a different outlook on life. Something may be nothing but a disaster and significant disappointment to you, but it may be pleasant to someone else. This particular someone else can help you unravel some knots in your task or even give you a fresh perspective you wouldn't have thought about.

What happened on this day?

According to Admiral Leahy, 'Potsdam had brought into sharp world focus the struggle of to great ideas – the Anglo-Saxon democratic principles of government and the aggressive and expansionist police-state tactics of Stalinist Russia. It was the beginning of the 'cold war.'

Truman got Stalin's commitment to enter into war against Japan in August.

The president left the Little White House in Babelsberg. He flew to Plymouth, England, and had lunch with Limy King. The king believed in the bomb.

Tibbets and Ferebee went over their plan for Hiroshima to get the perfect spot for the bomb. Everyone, including LeMay, agree Hiroshima was a perfect choice. They were going to fly down to drop the bomb at 31,000 feet above the city to prevent crosswinds from moving the bomb. Their aiming point was the Aioi Bridge.

COUNTDOWN: 3 DAYS
August 3, 1945
Washington, D.C.

Key Takeaways

1. War makes you understand what's important, what's necessary, and what's not important at all.

Learn to read beyond what people say or do into the intentions behind what has been said or done. Your boss might be hard on you because they believe in you.

What happened on this day?

Kauffman was to deliver a sealed envelope in person to Admiral Randall Jacobs, head of Navy Personnel.

He knew of Operation Olympic: the first phase of the invasion of Japan. He also knew of Operation Coronet.

He was given two weeks leave.

COUNTDOWN: 2 DAYS

August 4, 1964

Hiroshima

Key Takeaways

2. No matter how many times you hear the word 'NO' keep trying until you get what you want.
3. Don't get used to disappointment or negative thoughts.
4. Live each day like it's your last.
5. Live with a purpose.

Life is a risk. Each day we live through, there are a bunch of things that could go wrong and lead to death. Don't be afraid to live out the risk even in the face of death.

Your mind is yours and you're smart. You can think of a way out even when it seems obvious that there's no way.

What happened on this day?

Hideko and her friend Miyoshi had written letters to their mothers to come get them. Their mothers arrived and picked them. They simply wanted to go home. They agreed to go back to Hiroshima on Sunday August 5.

The teams chosen to bomb Hiroshima were given their briefing. They were debriefed and for the first time they had an idea of the effect the bomb would have.

COUNTDOWN: 1 DAY

August 5, 1945

Tinian

Key Takeaways

1. There can never be too much information for a task.
2. You can't be too prepared.
3. The safest option may be dangerous for an individual, but if it puts more lives out of risk than it would put more lives at risk, then it's safer for everyone.
4. Following your instinct is a way to survive and get the best result in hard times. It may mean going past authority or order.
5. Never rule out anything.
6. Build good memories with people.
7. Learn to see from other people's perspectives. This helps you understand them better and gives room for less fights, rancor and bickering.

Get facts and every other information right. Your life and the life of others may just depend on it.

No man is an island. We all need people from different fields and walks of life to come up with something entirely novel and solve the new challenges.

Learn to appreciate the effort of others. You may not fully understand what they do, but seeing the result from their work should make you appreciate them.

If you know what brings you luck, go ahead with it. It just might be your lifesaver. It might be a name, what you eat, a prayer, or anything you do that works as your lucky charm. If you believe in it, it just might work for you.

What happened on this day?

The team had to be sure they had favorable weather.

They chose August 6 as the day to drop the bomb.

Parsons was worried about taking off with a fully armed atomic bomb on board. He volunteered to arm the plane's bomb while they were in the air for the safety of the bomb and island.

Everything was put in place: planes were fueled and greased, guns were loaded and tested, radio and radar sets were tuned and checked, bombsights, autopilots, and compasses were calibrated.

Tibbets named the plane after his mother, and Lewis was angry.

There were seven crews involved. Some of them were able to eat, and others were too tense that they couldn't eat.

Tibbets made sure Beser had company: William Lawrence.

Scientist Ed Doll gave Beser a folded piece of rice paper with a line of numbers for the radio frequency the bomb would

use as it fell. He was instructed to swallow it in case of
eventualities.

COUNTDOWN: 9 HOURS, 15 MINUTES

August 6, 1945

Tinian

Key Takeaways

1. You can achieve a lot if you're calm.
2. Take every mission or task as your last chance to prove yourself. Give it your best shot.
3. Even though you can't be prepared enough, make sure you do your job, obey orders. Don't cut corners or take chances.
4. Listen carefully to instructions. Don't assume what you heard or didn't hear. Clarify whatever you aren't sure of so you don't work with your thoughts or feelings.

If you take in your practice and learn well, you'll be fine. The day to practice what you've learned will finally come and you'll do well.

What happened at this time?

Each man got a pair of adjustable arc welders' lenses and they were warned not to look at the flash of light with their naked eyes.

They had cyanide capsules they could swallow in case they fell into the hands of the enemy.

COUNTDOWN: 9 HOURS

Key Takeaways

1. Never underestimate the power of prayer. Prayer doesn't hurt.

If you speak with others about what you feel or what you're going through, you'll find out there are other people with similar issues as yours.

What happened at this time?

Captain William Downey, a Lutheran chaplain, led the team in prayers before they took off.

Tibbets was really tense and almost afraid. He couldn't eat. Beser ate a heavy meal.

COUTDOWN: 8 HOURS

Key Takeaways

1. Do your work and carry out tasks like a perfectionist would. Everything should be ready and spotless.
2. As a leader, make sure your work is neatly organized.

What happened at this time?

After breakfast, Tibbets and his crew went to their quarters to pick what they needed.

Van Kirk had the trip mapped out in his mind and would use the stars to navigate the plane most of the way.

Ferebee made sure there were no glitches with his Norden bomb sight.

COUNTDOWN: 7 HOURS 38 MINIUTES

What happened at this time?

The three weather planes took off.

The emergency plane that was to stand by at Iwo Jima in case the strike plane faltered also took off.

COUNTDOWN: 7 HOURS, 10 MINUTES

Key Takeaways

1. As much as you can, encourage everyone on your team.
2. Everyone needs some form of encouragement and no one is too small or too big to give encouragement.

What happened at this time?

As the Enola Gay crew members were about to board, they found their plane was surrounded by photographers, filmmakers and well-wishers according to General Grove's idea.

They took pictures and Lewis rounded up the crewmen.

COUNTDOWN: 7 HOURS 5 MINUTES

What happened at this time?

The plane carried an extra 15,000 pounds of weight to weigh 150,000.

The plane also carried fuel to offset the weight of Little Boy. Without the balance, takeoff would be impossible.

The plane was too heavy and too slow but it took off.

COUNTDOWN: 6 HOURS, 30 MINUTES

Key Takeaways

- When you're under a lot of pressure, do all you can to stay calm. That's the only way to get things done.

What happened at this time?

Parsons began to work and armed Little Boy. He was nervous but did his job in twenty minutes.

COUNTDOWN: 3 HOURS, 30 MINUTES

What happened at this time?

The other planes met up with Enola Gay over Iwo Jima and they set courses for Japan.

Lewis was writing his observations in a log for William Laurence.

COUNTDOWN: 2 HOURS 15 MINUTES

What happened at this time?

Tibbets informed them they were carrying the world's first atomic bomb and that the bomb was live.

Beser was to record their reaction when the bomb was dropped.

COUNTDOWN: 51 MINUTES

What happened at this time?

The weather planes flew ahead to ensure the weather was clear and the target choice was Hiroshima.

COUNTDOWN: 25 MINUTES

Key Takeaways
- Understand your plans and map and stick to it.

What happened at this time?

The crew noted the sky was clear.

COUNTDOWN: 10 MINUTES

What happened at this time?

The plane was at an altitude of 31,060 feet with airspeed of 200 miles when they saw Hiroshima and spotted the Aioi Bridge.

COUNTDOWN: 3 MINUTES
What happened at this time?

Ferebee ensured they were on target.

COUNTDOWN: 1 MINUTE
What happened at this time?

They put on their glasses.

COUNTDOWN: 58 SECONDS
What happened at this time?

The T-shaped Aioi Bridge was in clear range.

COUNTDOWN: 43 SECONDS
What happened at this time?

Ferebee pushed the button and released the bomb. The bomb dropped at 131,060 feet from the bridge.

COUNTDOWN: FIRESTORM

Prepare your kids for emergencies. For example, if you live in a place prone to earthquakes, teach them what to do to protect themselves.

After you've done your job well, celebrate your victory.

Even if you're the leader, give room for others to show their skills. No rule says leaders must lead from the front all the time. Give a place for others to be part of history.

As a leader, make choices that favor your people. You don't have to remain obstinate and stubborn because your people will bear the consequence of your action.

Be polite and respect people.

EPILOGUE

When making decisions, there will always be the right sides and implications for your choices. Your decisions will give room for better decisions or worse choices, depending on which kind you make.

Be sure of the decisions you make and stand by it.

CPSIA information can be obtained
at www.ICGtesting.com
Printed in the USA
BVHW031118100720
583342BV00004B/248

9 781952 639203